Trombone

Muscle Memory Exercises for Band

by Randy & Ami Kulik

P.O. Box 517   Glenmoore, PA 19343
Voice: 610-942-2370   Fax: 610-942-0660
Email: info@nemusicpub.com   ♪   Web: www.nemusicpub.com
1 2 3 4 5 6 7 8 17 16 15 14 13 12 11 10
Printed in the United States of America

Copyright © 2010 by Northeastern Music Publications, Inc.
All rights reserved. This book may not be reproduced by any means, whole
or in part, without written permission from the publisher.

Layout & Design by RoLin Graphics

Introduction

Muscle Memory is a concept that allows you to be an active participant in your musical education. If you were like us when we were kids, we would totally zone out every time our directors asked us to look at the key signature after we played a wrong note on our instruments! It's okay. It's not your fault! We wanted our directors to tell us what we were doing wrong. The *Muscle Memory Method* will teach you what to do.

- Muscle Memory allows you to create your scales and key signatures with the scale worksheets and develop the physical skills to play your scales accurately. The worksheets will also help you understand key signatures. You will be able to read music better.

    Look for the "brain" for memory tips in each lesson.

    Sharps= **F**at **C**ats **G**o **D**own **A**lleys **E**ating **B**irds

    Flats= **BEAD G**reat **C**hicago **F**ire

- Through the *Muscle Memory* physical activities, you will be shown a way to correct your mistakes and make it easier to play your band music.

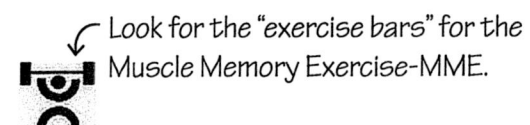

    Look for the "exercise bars" for the Muscle Memory Exercise-MME.

- The *Practice to Performance* exercises are designed to help you learn to play your scales from memory.

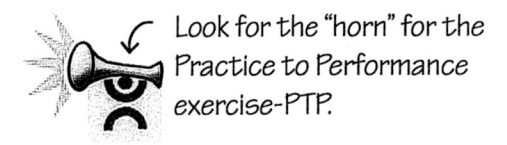

    Look for the "horn" for the Practice to Performance exercise-PTP.

- The *Practice to Performance* chorales will give you a chance to practice your PTP exercises with your full band or a small group.

    Your band director will decide how to play these.

    PTP Chorale

    Traditional Chorale

    Melody in Bass Chorale

- At the end of the book, you will find all the major scales to help you practice.

Trombone

After a little practice with this book you'll be able to play your scales more easily and in less time. You'll play the right notes more often because YOU will know how to correct your mistakes. Band will be more fun for you because you will know what you're doing. You'll be able to think about making music instead of worrying about playing wrong notes and your band director will be happy because you will be playing the right notes and reading music. Have fun!

Ami and Randy Kulik

Where to find it...

Page
- 2. Introduction
- 4. Key Signatures
- 5. Concert E♭ Major Scale
- 6. Concert A♭ Major Scale
- 7. Concert D♭ Major Scale
- 8. Concert G♭ Major Scale
- 9. Concert C♭ Major Scale
- 10. Concert B♭ Major Scale
- 11. Concert F Major Scale
- 12. Concert C Major Scale
- 13. Concert G Major Scale
- 14. Concert D Major Scale
- 15. Concert A Major Scale
- 16. Concert E Major Scale
- 17. Concert E♭ Chromatic
- 18. Concert B Major Scale (Enharmonic C♭)
- 19. Concert F♯ Major Scale Enharmonic G♭)
- 20. Concert C♯ Major Scale (Enharmonic D♭)
- 21. PTP Exercises for All Keys
- 23. All Major Scales and the Chromatic Scale

Trombone

Key Signature Rules

Order of Flats: B♭, E♭, A♭, D♭, G♭, C♭ F♭

BEAD **G**reat **C**hicago **F**ire

KEY SIGNATURE – FLAT RULE:

Go through the order of flats until you get to the name of your key and add one more. That will give you all the flats in the key signature.

EXAMPLE: Key of A♭
  Say the flats: B♭ – E♭ –(A♭)– add one more – D♭
  The key of A♭ has four flats: B♭, E♭, A♭, D♭

Key of:	Flats
F (1♭)	B♭
B♭ (2♭)	B♭, E♭
E♭ (3♭)	B♭ E♭ A♭
A♭ (4♭)	B♭ E♭ A♭ D♭
D♭ (5♭)	B♭ E♭ A♭ D♭ G♭
G♭ (6♭)	B♭ E♭ A♭ D♭ G♭ C♭
C♭ (7♭)	B♭ E♭ A♭ D♭ G♭ C♭ F♭

Order of Sharps: F#, C#, G#, D#, A#, E#, B#

Fat **C**ats **G**o **D**own **A**lleys **E**ating **B**irds

KEY SIGNATURE – SHARP RULE:

Name the sharp that's ½ step lower than the name of your key, and that's the last sharp in the key signature.

EXAMPLE: Key of D
  The sharp that is ½ step lower = C#
  The key of D has two sharps: F#, C#

Key of:	Sharps
G (1#)	F#
D (2#)	F# C#
A (3#)	F# C# G#
E (4#)	F# C# G# D#
B (5#)	F# C# G# D# A#
F# (6#)	F# C# G# D# A# E#
C# (7#)	F# C# G# D# A# E# B#

Memory Tip

Key of E♭: **Repeat to yourself or out loud:** "E♭ has 3 flats, E♭ has 3 flats – B♭, E♭, A♭"

Look for these Memory Tips in each lesson.

The 1st note of the scale is the "name of your scale"

Name of **your** scale _____

Name the notes of the Scale:
___ ___ ___ ___ ___ ___ ___ ___

4

BEAD Great **C**hicago **F**ire
Go through the order of flats until you get to the name of your key and add one more. That will give you all the flats in the key signature.

The Trombone is a concert pitch instrument.
The "concert pitch" is the name of your scale.

Concert E♭ Major Scale

Scale Work Sheet

Concert Pitch _____

Name of your scale
_____

Name the notes of the Scale:
___ ___ ___ ___ ___ ___ ___ ___

Key Signature : Name the flats

___ ___ ___

1. Write the key signature, measure bars and choose a time signature.
2. Write the scale using music notation. Use different note values to create a scale song.

Muscle Memory Exercise (MME): Concert E♭

1. <u>Without playing</u> your instrument, Practice slide positions **G** to **A♭**.
2. <u>Without playing</u> your instrument Practice slide positions **A♭** to **B♭**.
3. Practice the MME [**G-A♭-B♭-A♭-G**] 4 times on your instrument.

Practice to Performance (PTP)

1. Play the PTP exercise 4 times.
2. Turn to page 21 and play the E♭ PTP exercise #3.

Memory Tip

Key of E♭: **Repeat to yourself or out loud:**
E♭ has 3 flats, E♭ has 3 flats – B♭ E♭ A♭

PTP Chorale

Traditional Chorale

Melody in Bass Chorale

Trombone

BEAD Great Chicago Fire
Go through the order of flats until you get to the name of your key and add one more. That will give you all the flats in the key signature.

Concert A♭ Major Scale

Scale Work Sheet

Concert Pitch _____

Name of your scale
_____

Name the notes of the Scale:
___ ___ ___ ___ ___ ___ ___ ___

Key Signature : Name the flats
___ ___ ___ ___

1. Write the key signature, measure bars and choose a time signature.
2. Write the scale using music notation. Use different note values to create a scale song.

Muscle Memory Exercise (MME): Concert A♭
1. <u>Without playing</u> your instrument, Practice slide positions **C** to **D♭**.
2. <u>Without playing</u> your instrument Practice slide positions **D♭** to **E♭**.
3. Practice the MME [**C -D♭-E♭-D♭-C**] 4 times on your instrument.

Practice to Performance (PTP)
1. Play the PTP exercise 4 times.
2. Turn to page 21 and play the **A♭** PTP exercise #4.

Memory Tip
Key of A♭: *Repeat to yourself or out loud:* A♭ has 4 flats, A♭ has 4 flats – B♭ E♭ A♭ D♭

PTP Chorale

Traditional Chorale

Melody in Bass Chorale

Trombone

BEAD Great **C**hicago **F**ire
Go through the order of flats until you get to the name of your key and add one more. That will give you all the flats in the key signature.

Concert D♭ Major Scale

Scale Work Sheet

Concert Pitch _____

Name of your scale

_____

Name the notes of the Scale:

___ ___ ___ ___ ___ ___ ___ ___

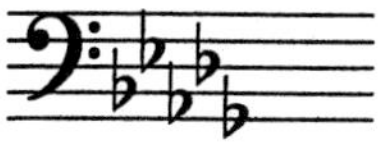

Key Signature :
Name the flats

___ ___ ___ ___ ___

1. Write the key signature, measure bars and choose a time signature.
2. Write the scale using music notation. Use different note values to create a scale song.

Muscle Memory Exercise (MME): Concert D♭

1. <u>Without playing</u> your instrument, Practice slide positions *F* to *G♭*.
2. <u>Without playing</u> your instrument Practice slide positions *G♭* to *A♭*.
3. Practice the MME [*F-G♭-A♭-G♭-F*] 4 times on your instrument.

Practice to Performance (PTP)

1. Play the PTP exercise 4 times.
2. Turn to page 21 and play the *D♭* PTP exercise #5.

Memory Tip

Key of D♭: **Repeat to yourself or out loud:**
D♭ has 5 flats, D♭ has 5 flats – B♭ E♭ A♭ D♭ G♭

PTP Chorale

Traditional Chorale

Melody in Bass Chorale

7

Trombone

Concert G♭ Major Scale

BEAD Great Chicago Fire
Go through the order of flats until you get to the name of your key and add one more. That will give you all the flats in the key signature.

Scale Work Sheet

Concert Pitch _____

Name of your scale
_____

Name the notes of the Scale:
___ ___ ___ ___ ___ ___ ___ ___

Key Signature: Name the flats
___ ___ ___ ___ ___ ___

1. Write the key signature, measure bars and choose a time signature.
2. Write the scale using music notation. Use different note values to create a scale song.

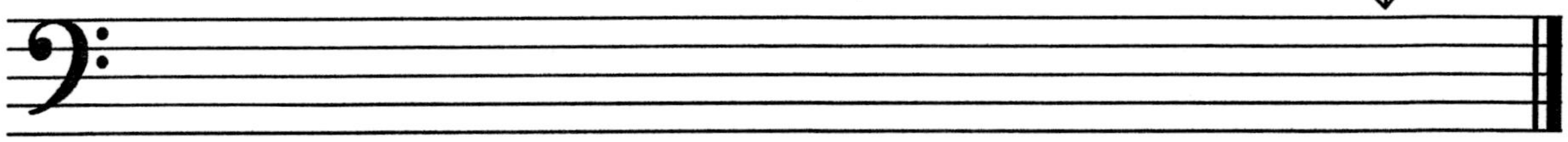

Muscle Memory Exercise (MME): Concert G♭

1. <u>Without playing</u> your instrument, Practice slide positions *B♭* to *C♭*.
2. <u>Without playing</u> your instrument Practice slide positions *C♭* to *D♭*.
3. Practice the MME [*B♭-C♭-D♭-C♭-B♭*] 4 times on your instrument.

Practice to Performance (PTP)

1. Play the PTP exercise 4 times.
2. Turn to page 21 and play the *G♭* PTP exercise #6.

Memory Tip

Key of G♭: *Repeat to yourself or out loud:*
G♭ has 6 flats, G♭ has 6 flats – B♭ E♭ A♭ D♭ G♭ C♭

PTP Chorale

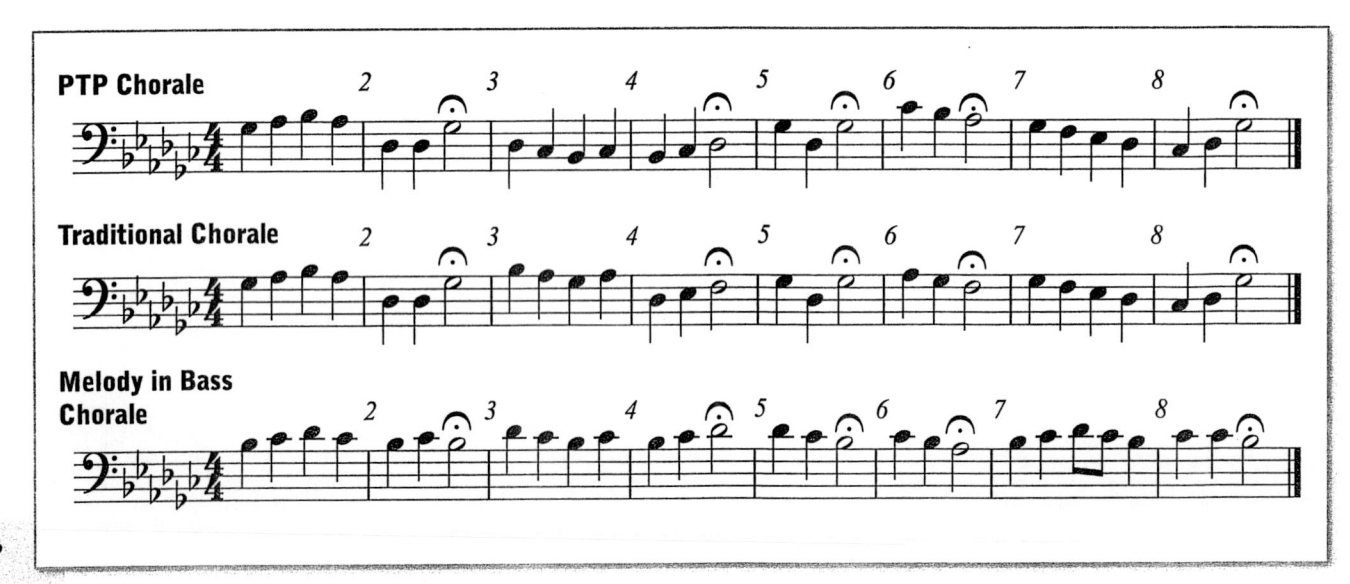

Traditional Chorale

Melody in Bass Chorale

8

Trombone

Concert C♭ Major Scale

BEAD Great **C**hicago **F**ire
Go through the order of flats until you get to the name of your key and add one more. That will give you all the flats in the key signature.

Scale Work Sheet

Concert Pitch _____

Name of your scale

_____

Name the notes of the Scale:

___ ___ ___ ___ ___ ___ ___ ___

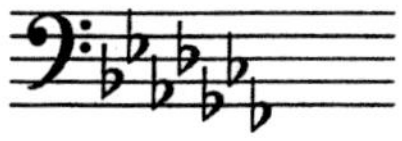

Key Signature : Name the flats

___ ___ ___ ___ ___ ___ ___

1. Write the key signature, measure bars and choose a time signature.
2. Write the scale using music notation. Use different note values to create a scale song.

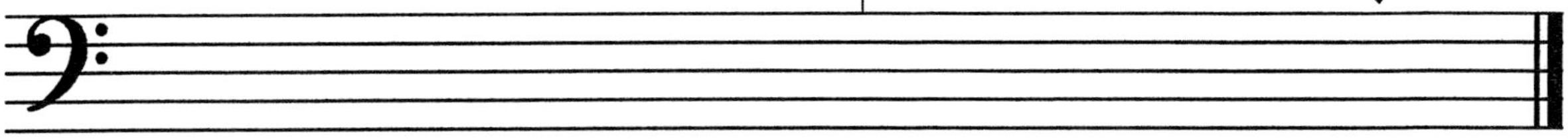

Muscle Memory Exercise (MME): Concert C♭

1. <u>Without playing</u> your instrument, Practice slide positions E♭ to F♭.
2. <u>Without playing</u> your instrument Practice slide positions F♭ to G♭.
3. Practice the MME [E♭-F♭-G♭-F♭-E♭] 4 times on your instrument.

Practice to Performance (PTP)

1. Play the PTP exercise 4 times.
2. Turn to page 21 and play the C♭ PTP exercise #7.

Memory Tip

Key of C♭: **Repeat to yourself or out loud:**
C♭ has 7 flats, C♭ has 7 flats
– B♭ E♭ A♭ D♭ G♭ C♭ F♭
I "C" (see) all flats.

PTP Chorale

Traditional Chorale

Melody in Bass Chorale

9

Trombone

BEAD **G**reat **C**hicago **F**ire
Go through the order of flats until you get to the name of your key and add one more. That will give you all the flats in the key signature.

Concert B♭ Major Scale

Scale Work Sheet

Concert Pitch _____

Name of your scale

_____

Name the notes of the Scale:

___ ___ ___ ___ ___ ___ ___ ___

Key Signature: Name the flats

___ ___

1. Write the key signature, measure bars and choose a time signature.
2. Write the scale using music notation. Use different note values to create a scale song.

Muscle Memory Exercise (MME): Concert B♭

1. <u>Without playing</u> your instrument, Practice slide positions **G** to **A** natural (♮).
2. <u>Without playing</u> your instrument Practice slide positions **A♮** to **B♭**.
3. Practice the MME [**G-A♮-B♭-A♮-G**] 4 times on your instrument.

Memory Tip

Key of B♭: **Repeat to yourself or out loud:**
B♭ has 2 flats, B♭ has 2 flats – B♭ E♭

Practice to Performance

1. Play the PTP exercise 4 times.
2. Turn to page 21 and play the B♭ PTP exercise #2.

PTP Chorale

Traditional Chorale

Melody in Bass Chorale

Trombone

Concert F Major Scale

BEAD Great Chicago Fire
Go through the order of flats until you get to the name of your key and add one more. That will give you all the flats in the key signature.

Scale Work Sheet

Concert Pitch _____

Name of your scale
_____

Name the notes of the Scale:
___ ___ ___ ___ ___ ___ ___ ___

Key Signature : Name the flat
___

1. Write the key signature, measure bars and choose a time signature.
2. Write the scale using music notation. Use different note values to create a scale song.

Muscle Memory Exercise (MME): Concert F
1. <u>Without playing</u> your instrument, Practice slide positions *D* to *E* natural (♮).
2. <u>Without playing</u> your instrument Practice slide positions *E♭* to *F*.
3. Practice the MME [*D-E♭-F-E♭-D*] 4 times on your instrument.

Memory Tip
Key of F: *Repeat to yourself or out loud:*
F has 1 flat, F has 1 flat–B♭

Practice to Performance (PTP)
1. Play the PTP exercise 4 times.
2. Turn to page 21 and play the **F** PTP exercise #1.

PTP Chorale

Traditional Chorale

Melody in Bass Chorale

11

Trombone

Concert C Major Scale

Scale Work Sheet

Concert Pitch ____

Name of your scale

_____

Name the notes of the Scale:

___ ___ ___ ___ ___ ___ ___ ___

1. Write the key signature, measure bars and choose a time signature.
2. Write the scale using music notation. Use different note values to create a scale song.

Muscle Memory Exercise (MME): Concert C

1. <u>Without playing</u> your instrument, Practice slide positions **A** to **B** natural (♮).
2. <u>Without playing</u> your instrument Practice slide positions **B♮** to **C**.
3. Practice the MME [**A-B♮-C-B♮-A**] 4 times on your instrument.

Memory Tip

Key of C: **Repeat to yourself or out loud:**
I "C" (see) no sharps,
I "C" (see) no flats.

Practice to Performance (PTP)

1. Play the PTP exercise 4 times.
2. Turn to page 22 and play the **C** PTP exercise #1.

PTP Chorale

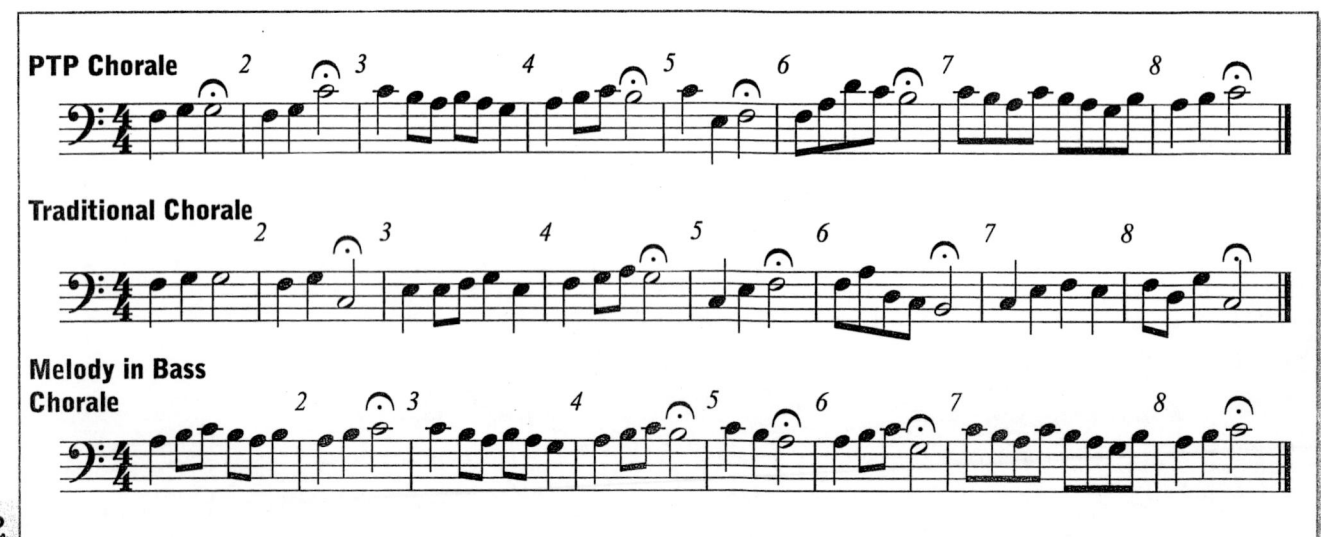

Traditional Chorale

Melody in Bass Chorale

12

Trombone

Concert G Major Scale

Fat Cats Go Down Alleys Eating Birds
Name the sharp that's ½ step lower than the name of your key, and that's the last sharp in the key signature.

Scale Work Sheet

Concert Pitch _____

Name of your scale
_____

Name the notes of the Scale:
___ ___ ___ ___ ___ ___ ___ ___

Key Signature : Name the sharp
_____

1. Write the key signature, measure bars and choose a time signature.
2. Write the scale using music notation. Use different note values to create a scale song.

Muscle Memory Exercise (MME): Concert G

1. <u>Without playing</u> your instrument, Practice slide positions *E* to *F#*.
2. <u>Without playing</u> your instrument Practice slide positions *F#* to *G*.
3. Practice the MME [*E-F#-G-F#-E*] 4 times on your instrument.

Memory Tip
Key of G: **Repeat to yourself or out loud:**
G has 1 sharp, G has 1 sharp – F#

Practice to Performance (PTP)

1. Play the PTP exercise 4 times.
2. Turn to page 22 and play the *G* PTP exercise #2.

PTP Chorale

Traditional Chorale

Melody in Bass Chorale

13

Trombone

Concert D Major Scale

Fat **C**ats **G**o **D**own **A**lleys **E**ating **B**irds
Name the sharp that's ½ step lower than the name of your key, and that's the last sharp in the key signature.

Scale Work Sheet

Concert Pitch _____

Name of your scale

_____

Name the notes of the Scale:

__ __ __ __ __ __ __ __

Key Signature: Name the sharps

___ ___

1. Write the key signature, measure bars and choose a time signature.
2. Write the scale using music notation. Use different note values to create a scale song.

Muscle Memory Exercise (MME): Concert D

1. <u>Without playing</u> your instrument, Practice slide positions *B* to *C♯*.
2. <u>Without playing</u> your instrument, Practice slide positions *C♯* to *D*.
3. Practice the MME [*B-C♯-D-C♯-B*] 4 times on your instrument.

Practice to Performance (PTP)

1. Play the PTP exercise 4 times.
2. Turn to page 22 and play the *D* PTP exercise #3.

Memory Tip

Key of D: *Repeat to yourself or out loud:* D has 2 sharps, D has 2 sharps – F♯ C♯

PTP Chorale

Traditional Chorale

Melody in Bass Chorale

14

Trombone

Concert A Major Scale

Fat Cats Go Down Alleys Eating Birds
Name the sharp that's ½ step lower than the name of your key, and that's the last sharp in the key signature.

Scale Work Sheet

Concert Pitch _____

Name of your scale
_____

Name the notes of the Scale:
___ ___ ___ ___ ___ ___ ___ ___

Key Signature : Name the sharps
___ ___ ___

1. Write the key signature, measure bars and choose a time signature.
2. Write the scale using music notation. Use different note values to create a scale song.

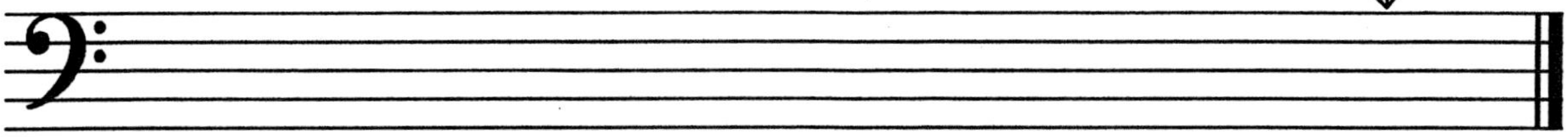

Muscle Memory Exercise (MME): Concert A

1. <u>Without playing</u> your instrument, Practice slide positions *F#* to *G#*.
2. <u>Without playing</u> your instrument Practice slide positions *G#* to *A*.
3. Practice the MME [*F#-G#-A-G#-F#*] 4 times on your instrument.

Practice to Performance (PTP)

1. Play the PTP exercise 4 times.
2. Turn to page 22 and play the *A* PTP exercise #4.

Memory Tip

Key of A: *Repeat to yourself or out loud:*
A has 3 sharps, A has 3 sharps – F# C# G#

PTP Chorale

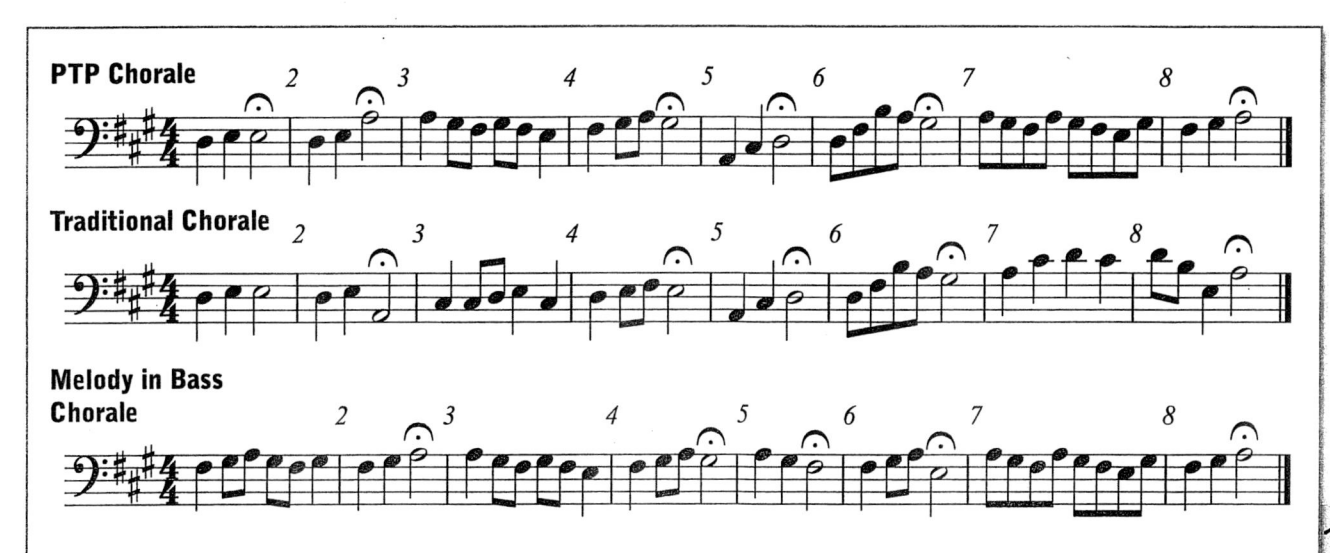

Traditional Chorale

Melody in Bass Chorale

15

Trombone

Fat Cats Go Down Alleys Eating Birds
Name the sharp that's ½ step lower than the name of your key, and that's the last sharp in the key signature.

Concert E Major Scale

Scale Work Sheet

Concert Pitch _____

Name of your scale

_____

Name the notes of the Scale:

___ ___ ___ ___ ___ ___ ___ ___

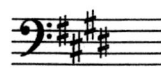

Key Signature: Name the sharps

___ ___ ___ ___

1. Write the key signature, measure bars and choose a time signature.
2. Write the scale using music notation. Use different note values to create a scale song.

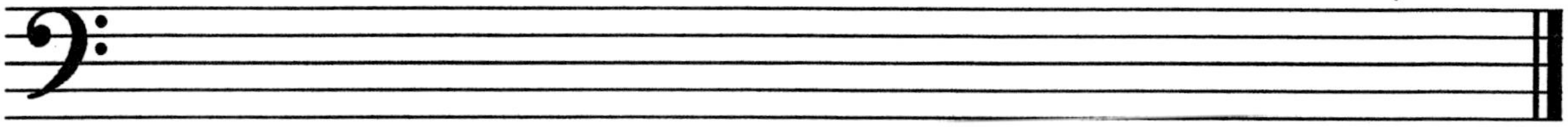

Muscle Memory Exercise (MME): Concert E

1. <u>Without playing</u> your instrument, Practice slide positions C# to D#.
2. <u>Without playing</u> your instrument Practice slide positions D# to E.
3. Practice the MME [C#-D#-E-D#-C#] 4 times on your instrument.

Practice to Performance (PTP)

1. Play the PTP exercise 4 times.
2. Turn to page 22 and play the *E* PTP exercise #5.

Memory Tip
Key of E: **Repeat to yourself or out loud:**
E has 4 sharps, E has 4 sharp – F# C# G# D#

PTP Chorale

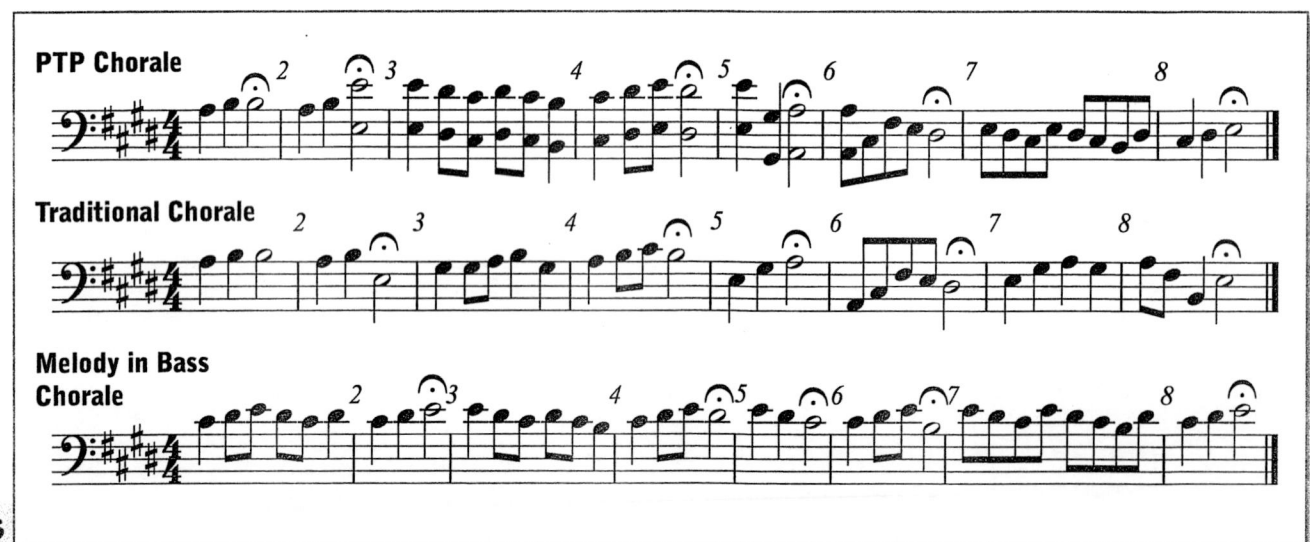

Traditional Chorale

Melody in Bass Chorale

Trombone

Concert E♭ Chromatic Scale

BEAD Great Chicago Fire
Go through the order of flats until you get to the name of your key and add one more. That will give you all the flats in the key signature.

Concert Pitch ____

Name of your scale
_____

Key Signature:
Name the flats
___ ___ ___

Name the notes of the ascending (going up) chromatic scale, followed by the descending chromatic scale (going down). Use your enharmonic relationship chart if you need help.

___ ___ ___ ___ ___ ___ ___ ___ ___ ___ ___ ___ ___

___ ___ ___ ___ ___ ___ ___ ___ ___ ___ ___ ___ ___

1. Write the key signature, measure bars and choose a time signature.
2. Write the scale using music notation. Use different note values to create a scale song.

Scale Work Sheet

Memory Tip

Enharmonic Relationships

C♯=D♭ | D♯=E♭ | E=F♭ | E♯=F | F♯=G♭ | G♯=A♭ | A♯=B♭ | B=C♭ | B♯=C

Practice to Performance (PTP)
1. Play PTP exercise 4 times.

17

Trombone

Fat Cats Go Down Alleys Eating Birds
Name the sharp that's ½ step lower than the name of your key, and that's the last sharp in the key signature.

Concert B Major Scale
(Enharmonic C♭)

Concert Pitch _____

Name of your scale

_____

Name the notes of the Scale:

___ ___ ___ ___ ___ ___ ___ ___

Key Signature:
Name the sharps

___ ___ ___ ___ ___

1. Write the key signature, measure bars and choose a time signature.
2. Write the scale using music notation. Use different note values to create a scale song.

Scale Work Sheet

Memory Tip
Key of B: **Repeat to yourself or out loud:**
B has 5 sharps, B has 5 sharp – F♯ C♯ G♯ D♯ A♯

Muscle Memory Exercise (MME): Concert B
1. <u>Without playing</u> your instrument, Practice slide positions *G♯* to *A♯*.
2. <u>Without playing</u> your instrument Practice slide positions *A♯* to *B*.
3. Practice the MME [*G♯-A♯-B-A♯-G♯*] 4 times on your instrument.

Practice to Performance (PTP)
1. Play the PTP exercise 4 times.
2. Turn to page 22 and play the *B* PTP exercise #6

18

Trombone

Concert F# Major Scale
(Enharmonic G♭)

Fat Cats Go Down Alleys Eating Birds
Name the sharp that's ½ step lower than the name of your key, and that's the last sharp in the key signature.

Concert Pitch _____

Name of your scale

_____

Name the notes of the Scale:

___ ___ ___ ___ ___ ___ ___

Key Signature : Name the sharps

___ ___ ___ ___ ___ ___

1. Write the key signature, measure bars and choose a time signature.
2. Write the scale using music notation. Use different note values to create a scale song.

Scale Work Sheet

Memory Tip

Key of F#: **Repeat to yourself or out loud:**
F# has 6 sharps, F# has 6 sharps – F# C# G# D# A# E#

Muscle Memory Exercise (MME): Concert F#
1. <u>Without playing</u> your instrument, practice slide positions *D#* to *E#*.
2. <u>Without playing</u> your instrument practice fingering *E#* to *F#*.
3. Practice the MME [*D#-E#-F#-E#-D#*] 4 times on your instrument.

Practice to Performance (PTP)
1. Play the PTP exercise 4 times.
2. Turn to page 22 and play the *F#* PTP exercise #7

Trombone

Fat Cats Go Down Alleys Eating Birds
Name the sharp that's ½ step lower than the name of your key, and that's the last sharp in the key signature.

Concert C♯ Major Scale
(Enharmonic D♭)

Concert Pitch ____

Name of your scale

_____

Name the notes of the Scale:

__ __ __ __ __ __ __ __

Key Signature : Name the sharps

__ __ __ __ __ __ __

1. Write the key signature, measure bars and choose a time signature.
2. Write the scale using music notation. Use different note values to create a scale song.

Scale Work Sheet

Memory Tip
Key of C♯: **Repeat to yourself or out loud:**
C♯ has 7 sharps, C♯ has 7 sharps – F♯ C♯ G♯ D♯ A♯ E♯ B♯.
I "C" (see) all sharps.

Muscle Memory Exercise (MME): Concert C♯
1. <u>Without playing</u> your instrument, Practice slide positions A♯ to B♯.
2. <u>Without playing</u> your instrument Practice slide positions B♯ to C♯.
3. Practice the MME [A♯-B♯-C♯-B♯-A♯] 4 times on your instrument.

Practice to Performance (PTP)
1. Play the PTP exercise 4 times.
2. Turn to page 22 and play the C♯ PTP exercise #8.

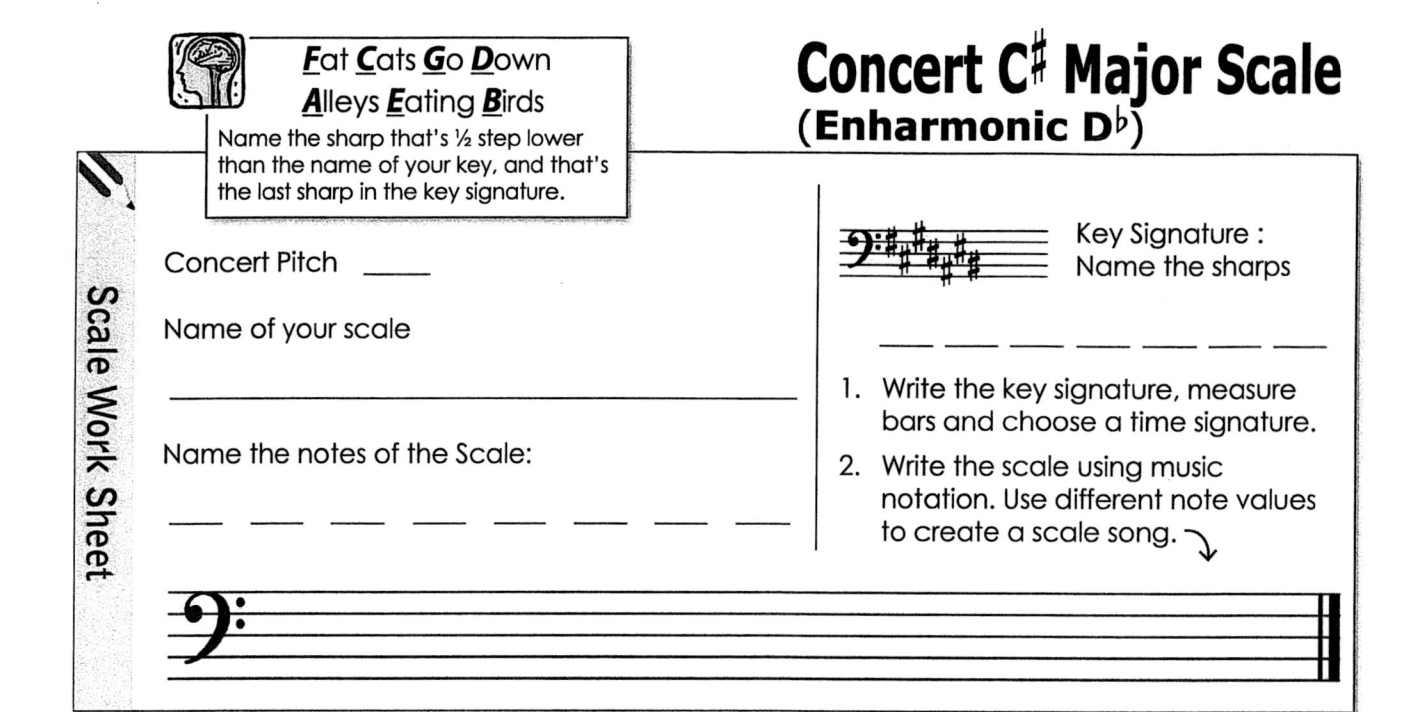

20

PTP Exercises for all Keys

Concert F

1.

Concert B♭

2.

Concert E♭

3.

Concert A♭

4.

Concert D♭

5.

Concert G♭

6.

Concert C♭

7.

Trombone

Trombone

PTP Exercises for all Keys

Concert C

1.

Concert G

2.

Concert D

3.

Concert A

4.

Concert E

5.

Concert B

6.

Concert F#

7.

Concert C#

8.

22

All Major Scales and the Chromatic Scale

F Major

1.

B♭ Major

2.

E♭ Major

3.

A♭ Major

4.

D♭ Major

5.

G♭ Major

6.

C♭ Major (enharmonic B)

7.

E♭ Chromatic Scale

8.

All Major Scales (continued)